Drunk
Love
Sober
Death

Poetry by Jade Jackson

Legal

© Jade Jackson 2020 including content, cover image and design.

First published with Apple Books in 2020. Self-published.

This print edition ISBN: 978-0-6488132-1-7
Also available:
ePub edition, ISBN: 978-0-6488132-0-0
Audiobook edition, ISBN: 978-0-6488132-3-1

Please do not amend anything, reproduce, share or transmit by any means any part of this publication, without prior written permission from the author. It is forbidden to publish, sell or make available to sell any part of this publication in part or in whole including its images and cover design, except a brief extract (which must be attributed to "Jade Jackson") for the purpose of a review, without prior written permission from the author.

This is a work of fiction. Any similarity to persons living or dead or actual locations is purely coincidental and no harm or offence was intended. Whilst all reasonable care was taken when preparing this book to ensure this publication is free of errors, the author makes no warranty and to the maximum extent permitted, disclaims all liability from its use.

About the Author

Jade Jackson is an Author, Podcaster and Photographer, based in the Blue Mountains, Australia. He's published a play, *Compass* along with a novella and he's also written hundreds of travel articles.

He produces three podcasts, *Jade Talks Travel*, *Jade Talks Cheap Flights* and *Jade Talks Stuff*.

Travel and Poetry drive's him, and he loves the sound of words, often combining foreign words or phrases in his everyday speech because they are more pleasing to the ear than their English equivalents.

He's ever searching for that one place to call home, yet he is at home anywhere. You can find more of his works and connect with him via his website at:

www.jadejackson.com.au

Preface

"They are mere words which can mean everything or they can mean nothing, such is their power.
The spoken word, mightier. The whispered word, lighter. Keep your words precious beside you, they will win both wars and gold someday."

—Jade Jackson

Discovering poetry was akin to becoming fluent in a new language, overnight. Now I write poetry, as I breathe or blink. It's not something I do, it is me.

What started as awkward expressions, scribbled in pencil, influenced by rock stars and beat poets; brought purpose to my life. Besides capturing thoughts, reading aloud a beautiful poem that I've created brings immense joy and helps to keep me sane.

In 2013, I lost most of my written works in a house fire. However, my younger self hand wrote my favourite poems into several notebooks and gifted them to my closest friends.

The owner of one notebook, Emma, posted her copy back to me a few months after the fire, which I'm forever grateful for. Without which, this book would not have happened.

Re-reading those precious poems reignited the spark and reminded me I had written nothing substantial in several years.

When I wrote my play, *Compass*, I was alcohol free for nine months which resulted in exceptional clarity and productivity. So I trialled going alcohol free once more to find that same zest and dedication.

Within two weeks, I was writing again and I have not stopped.

It was from poetry that my writing grew to include songs, plays, novels, articles and podcasts.

This collection of poetry, *Drunk Love, Sober Death*, comprises two books.

Book one features poems written before I removed alcohol from my life. It's a journey which represents how alcohol affects the writing process.

Book two is everything that came from living a life, alcohol free; like a fog had lifted, this clarity allowed words to flow, and from this came evocative and powerful poems.

In 2019, I lost several friends and relatives and it was through grief; I learned a lot about life. Some of those lessons feature in a novel I'm working on, but in those endless dark days of grief, poetry was my saviour.

From drunken ramblings, to empty nights filled with broken emotions; for the first time, I present: *Drunk Love Sober Death*.

Read these poems aloud or listen to the audio version, to immerse yourself and experience them as I intended. Enjoy.

— Jade Jackson

Legal	4
About the Author	5
Preface	6
Book One	15
Scouring the city's roots	16
I went out walking	17
Can you see my smile	18
Powerless beats	19
Angel died…	20
I served her well	21
The Church walls bend	22
Her curls shiver	23
A fountain of days	24
Marriage celebrants	25
W/my nurturing silk	26
BLANK	27
Watch the Sunrise…	28
Our world so dark…	29
The pigeon lay…	30
The switch blade kisses	31
Out burned the lights	32
Grim reaper	33

Back door moans	34
Gentle kisses	35
The night was wet	36
A vast array	37
Fermented angel tears	38
I have the hand	40
The vent disguised	41
A smoking jazz singer	42
Along a dirt path	43
Inspiration is my host	44
A Botanist's dream	46
Riches	47
Wizard	48
Dictator	49
Unconcern	50
The General	51
We are all monsters	52
Gathering	53
I search the skies	54
Hovering	56
You are round	57
Dragon eyes	58

I'm a strange man	59
Spent to degrade	60
A Paris love	61
It's time for havoc	62
A weed	64
Where will we go?	66
There is a light	67
Chopping…churning	68
In your eyes	69
Tread softly	70
Unleashing dreams	71
Bleach stained smile	72
The future is pills	73
Pack up my bags	74
Spinning the other way	76
I thought I lost the urge	77
Your lover…	78
A halo surrounds	79
Give me some death	81
This is the windy city	82
Why do I feel?	84
I must arise	85

I'm being eaten	86
The only war I see	87
Makes me want to cry*	88
Book Two	89
This windy city	90
Rusty	91
W/a sigh	92
Veggie Burger Patty	93
Your rhymes	94
The smell of ink	95
Still here I am	98
Children seated	100
A round table	101
Pretending to read	102
Invisible	104
Shape shifting stairs	105
Today it's empty	106
Water smashing	108
Ancient leaves twisted	109
Looking at the moon	110
Flowered wall	111
Short cube	113

Lips dry	114
Lovely little thing	115
My heart tremors	116
Ostracised	118
The red zone	120
Half-baked face	123
Lake Hindmarsh	126
A cliff top	129
Thunderstorm blues	132
In a hate filled world	134
We're told to dream	136
I long for sweet kisses	138
The refugee	140
I starve	143
Cliff tops*	145
Memories tainted	147
Fireworks	149
W/clouds	151
Christmas in New York*	153
A wall	159
None of it matters*	162
The box	166

I expected answers	169
A blanket of softness	171
It hurts to think	173
Should have been a Mrs	175
Gone from my days	177
A dent in the dirt	181
Once a purpose lay	184
Across the ether	187
A pocket of wildness	188
We know nothing	189
With each heavy breath	191
Micro story #1	194
Micro story #2	195
Micro story #3	196
Micro story #4	197
Micro story #5	198
Afterward	200

Book One

Scouring the city's roots

Scouring the city's roots
dodging eight veins of lice I challenge the mood
of hormonal fluid.

A quiet mosaic
heightens the mystique
of hookers
    floating on pants.

Ingest this drug,
        this I do.
A car beep,
       heat,
          heartbeat.
Prepare thyself to induce the big sleep.

Grease food invokes sour moods and a quad box of
chicks inherit mindless feats.

I went out walking

I went out walking amongst the trees today,
I spoke to no one but me.

Then I found a special place,
of rainforest mist and a web of lace.

Can you see my smile

Can you see my smile unfold?
This I tell you,
can not be withheld.

Not today,
nor the morrow,
nor any happy day to follow.

Powerless beats

Powerless beats embalm my friend.
A padded cell ensures us well.

A subliminal breeze statically brews.
To those of no offence,
it serves no use.

We race around linoleum chalked floors —
we lose ourselves to all fours.

Fucked if you would
melt,
       nondescript the way I stood.

Pacing epileptics stride in turn
crippling my disease of defection.

Angel died...

Angel died,
lay soft
in dust.

Broken halo,
now turned to rust.
A false smile branded onto face,
like rigor mortis of a frozen lake.

Nothing inside left to burn.
Lament the death of my guardian.

I served her well

I served her well—the albino shell.
Nondescript of internal waves,
solitude, her defending ways.

Violet eyed teen sheds a destructive gaze
and snowflakes
tickle her ears and play.

The Church walls bend

The church walls bend with harmonious vibes,
luring men to a haven inside,
with angels, sirens.

A hall of guilt,
     a plaque of pain…
          of sorrow.

Where all is forgiven
until what comes tomorrow?

A heavenly voice poisons the air,
so I keep walking than hide in there.

Her curls shiver

Her curls shiver
to the passing train.

Her eyes don't notice,
her mind's slain.

A fountain of days

A fountain of days,
                erupts…
                          crying.

Only the few little people
                shelter its dying ways.

Bubbles repugnant, divide blue shades of green.

Marriage celebrants

Marriage celebrants gather to prey,
devising to drain,
capture the days.

Yet soon too late for the cascading haze
as rubble depicts
everlasting rage.

W/my nurturing silk

W/my nurturing silk,
I drink to sleep.
Warm
by a fire.
A flittering moth
I try to grasp.
My stupefied state
a ruthless beast,
too strong, mortifies.
Alone
with my bourbon and milk.

BLANK

BLANK

was my mind

before this time

until an angel vaporised.

Turning my life unto insane

and bringing me love without pain.

Watch the Sunrise...

Watch the sunrise over my enterprise.
Escaping.
Stage cry,
wilt not,
"have some pork pie."
Clashing sequined hard bodies appeasing.
Revealing thoughts of myself,
crushing a dead man and taunting.

Our world so dark…

Our world so dark and grey,
misery blankets this day.
Why do we feel?
Though it can be good,
mostly I think it's psychologically wrong.
Now our lifeblood be being,
yet misery still is grieving.

The pigeon lay...

The pigeon lay squished into the ground,
a toucan mug
smashed all around.

Basking neath the light,
of a moon envied bright.

There was a sound —
clinking...
just like
glasses tripping
on the wind,
so light.

This all became too much for me,
I opted to exit such obscurity.

The switch blade kisses

The switch blade kisses naked flesh,
after every shot.

Resurrect a mindless seam
which instigates the beauty queen.

Defiant throes
chundering blows
return messianic,
demonic
incessant lows.

"That girl is just so ripe," tending to a lover.

What they will force her to fantasize throughout
dehydrated dreams customised to a whimpering fire.

Crouched atop the pageant of desire.

Out burned the lights

Out burned the lights
                and fed me the dark.

Onwards we walked
                and bred crass remarks.

The band,
        they played on—piano, cello, vocals…
        hmm mellow.

I was wearing blue jeans if I remember correctly
for they tore me down.
                Yeah.

Grim reaper

Grim reaper of the insect world
dissolves all the snails with virgin salt.

Set aflame the disturbed flies,
floating adrift on the windowpane.

Set aflame the parasites,
burn them all to hell.

Try it, it's swell.

Back door moans

Back door moans with insidious views.
Creatures,
perturbed with features stroll misaligned.

Adorn the lover of Versileas*
draped with pristine livery.

Migrating music bends and grinds.
I lied.

Parading neath the sparkling rain.
A humid scent
scraping beyond the tarmac.

Clean,
this time of fear
from the billowing heat
shading my view; corrupting.

*Versileas (or Verse for short) was a fictional character in a story, that was lost in the fire.

Gentle kisses

Gentle kisses,
stale green breath,
naked wrath.

My holiness.
       My love is like a seafood dress.
A sight worth its time
yet, a smell undivine.

Flaking and falling,
twisted and stalling.
There are no words to speak anymore.

The night was wet

The night was wet,
black and white,
effervescent grey.
I was being watched
in a movie
in a subtle way.

A vast array

A vast array
swept in by wind
of emotions.

In the wake,
a ray of hope
in a sun filled lonely sky —
feels like a soft wet kiss
of first dawn.

But most of all
I am drawn
to a light,
shining endorphins.

Fermented angel tears

Fermented angel tears,
blood and the passing years,
have all their toll
on a poor, listless soul
and with that
goes all I trust.

Let's drink away, I must.

Grasping at my scabs
panting dribs and drabs.

I'm dripping then spilling
it looks I've been a killing.

Alas, my dearest
fear my greatest.
Blindness hides my latest hate
tiredness my greatest ache.

Sigh and with that
we must end this date.

I surrender to the heaving
powerful weight
and collapse beyond my closing fate.

Floating in a warm
unfound lake.

I have the hand

I have the hand of a spider's glove
smothering your face
with such unkind love.

The vent disguised

The vent disguised along all walls
breathes inside with open ears.

A brilliant flash
emits a scent of hash
and groupies lounging
panic, then rush.

A smoking jazz singer

There was a smoking jazz singer
I encountered the last evening.

Fair, a waif,
she moved me by just breathing.

Resembling a bird,
      the way she spasmodically moved her head
      in time to the beats
      generated by her fellow band members.

I'd like to kiss her thought I
because,
    I,
        eh,
            ah.
I love her,
she is the rain.

Along a dirt path

Along a dirt path
in the brisk, mottled shade.
I have only one shoe,
yet still I parade.

Still, I march on
down the treacherous pass,
where bees hum above
and a stream runs amuck.

Until such a time
when we come to the end.
Where we sit and drink
in our cool, calm Newfoundland.

Floating and gloating
in the bright green fun.

Washing away
with the crying fern.

Inspiration is my host

Inspiration is my host.
I'm a parasite
living like a ghost.

Eating sand and biting dust,
I am nothing
without lust.

I am nothing
in my life.
I am nothing
without life.

If you weren't so accepting,
I would not be existing.

Without a chance
to lay my eggs,
my wings won't spread.

I am nothing
in my life.
I am nothing
without life.

A Botanist's dream

It was a Botanist's dream
I left behind.

The sultry gallows evoked;
Crippled limbs
of deceased vines
and a cradle to mope in the night.

Riches

Riches, gold,
wealth and bitches
be all I'm not,
but to spend my hate on everything,
that is too late.

Wizard

Wizard —
king be seen.

Seeming
to relay the night.

Homing
as a rat with wings

Diseased.

Dictator

Dictator,
preacher,
and the (might be) reaper.

Sullen wolf
suffering breed
without heed.
The dexterous army spread fast and killed silently.

Their good karma left behind.

Unconcern

Unconcern
permeating
my ability.

Heartfelt pain
shading tears
beyond recognition.

In to our field
digesting my dreams.

Cherish
my post innocence
naïve flaunting;
cherish
my friend.

The General

The general recreates
a time-worn path.

Epitomising sadness,
evil hatred
and outstanding emotions.

Masculine visions
reveal feminine vulnerability.

Rape.
War cries,
try cannibalism.

Sifting pleas
and jungle sweat.

Smoke
brings forth
deaths tears.

We are all monsters

We are all monsters
hiding in our caves of skin.

You spoke too soon —
Shallow.

I watched you bleed
and heard you cry.

Together we sang
and all seemed fine.

An artist was painting
a Spanish child (in clay)
and a pianist distracts the workers
with chants.

Gathering

Gathering,
gathering,
gathering.
Everywhere is smothering.
Moulding, all of which it sees
especially plants
green with leaves.

I search the skies

I search the skies
in hopeless vain
wondering when
will it rain?

To bathe my soul
and purge my thoughts,
I'm wondering,
will it stop my taunts?

With high acidity
see it peeling away my skin,
removing me of doubt
and cleansing me all out.

I curse at all the filth
building up and hiding there.

Rid me of my veins with silt,
expanding
about to explode
everywhere.

The walls all around
splashed with blood and my flesh.
Specked with black dirt,
hatred and anguish.

There's my smile on the carpet,
my eyes are in the air,
I see myself,
everywhere.

Shrouded in dust,
devouring a path of greed,
leaving a wake of lust.

Hovering

Hovering just within view
an aurora,
in my sleeping room.

Glittering, dazzling,
burning too.
I painted the sky,
a stormy blue.

Splattered by rage
shadowed with laze.
My eye brought upon
this view for days.

You are round

You are round
to dissipate
blend your peers
expunge your hate.

I'd smoke my friends, given the chance.

Corrupted hairs
entwined,
resign
to cut your night
into another day.

Dragon eyes

Dragon eyes
weirdo pies
Greek god lies
I fantasize.

Bewildered woman
lost in skies
of flying flies,
penetrating blue vibes.

Manic panic
people inscribe
starting fires
and dousing wives.

This crowded jive
encasing my
all these prying eyes
parading throughout my hive.

I'm a strange man

I'm a strange man
in a modern land,
creating wonderful things
           when I can.

Passing and meeting people,
my raspy voice, greeting people.

The shoes I bear,
thoughts I wear
peculiar, almost rare.

A delicate taste
of the strangest race
twisted, basted
resigned, laced.

Spent to degrade

Spent to degrade,
putrid enrage
leave now
I need not to persuade.
Waving a flag,
velvet
crushed and glimmering.
Diligently, you seem
quite the less inspired.

A Paris love

A Paris love
emerged this time
from inserts,
        speeches
                and divine messages.

Polluting naked thoughts of a teen.
Sweetness reaches
everything she'd say.

It's time for havoc

It's time for havoc on the streets,
let's go out now.

We'll burn the tide
then run and hide
this to show majestic pride.

Shall we break glass?
Hey, let's strain the living,
and to traverse until the light
comes help from a trend in sight.

Music is my special friend
she wakes me up and I feel grand.

When all the rest alight
she sails forth
to make me feel all right.

'Cause music is my special friend.

She wears the walls,
that keep me here.
    Insane.

Sane.

A weed

What makes a weed a flower?
Used to me
        a withered devourer;
you're a weed,
you're a weed
and I'm a flower,
yet I taste sour.

What makes a weed a flower?
The seed?
      The looks I need,
           or reign by the hour?

I'm a weed,
I'm a weed.
You're a flower
and I'm the devouring, deflowering kind.

Of all the weeds
with all their power,
you're the beast
the pest of now.

No lulling, poisoned scent
removes me from your grip.
Showers veil
withering now
and all but left is zero.

Where will we go?

Where will we go today?
Just me,
       and your face I see when I close my eyes.

Where will we end up, if we follow our feet?

Will we land in a place
of birds and leaves?

Can we close our eyes and wander?
I wonder?

What do you think?
What do you feel?
We'll just keep walking
               and something will find us to do.

There is a light

There is a light
there is this day
where sacrificial happenings
enhance the way.

Out of my reach
and in every way,
I fall upon things
which carry me away.

Chopping...churning

Chopping and churning.
A sea in a teacup,
we drink the world
the foetus inside us.

Sipping,
tripping,
from our sea in a teacup.

In your eyes

In your eyes,
I float like a cloud.
United,
to the sky above.

Tread softly

Tread softly,
    whisper ever so lightly,
lest you wake
    beside this unrealistic dream.

Black in the night —
    this crazy haze
protecting my view;
corrupting.

Unleashing dreams

Unleashing dreams of previous thoughts.

Withholding emotions
kept locked in vaults.

Harsh vapours crowd my breath.
Floral addicts
        encrust.

Inventing poisoned lust.

Bleach stained smile

Bleach stained smile
with stinky breath.

Nicotine hair,
drowning coarse whine.

Barbaric yet zealous,
such a work of art.

Mourning shades,
she is wearing.
Dusky silk
she's weaving.

Musky scents
have been breaking,
shattered oceans
are falling.

The future is pills

The future is pills,
                gills,
                              and oil spills.

Plastic wrapped are the rolling hills.

Shimmering lights,
burning, unending.

With people infecting,
everywhere.

Pack up my bags

Pack up my bags
weighted down, full of sorrow.

Everyone is weeping, now that I am leaving.

I'm off to where the sun does not rise,
the trees bare, no leaves
and the only people always cry.

There is no reason to smile
where I'll end up.

Only misery
cause darkness
is all that's ever up.

There's no fun and games,
only bombing aeroplanes.

To dispel any fears
I wet my hands
and rid them of any wretched stinking germs.

Black and dirty,
they'll only add to my hurt.

I'm going now, Good Bye.
I'm off to where the sun does not rise,
the trees bare, no leaves,
and the only people always cry.

Spinning the other way

Spinning the other way out,
captivating all who's near or far,
before exploding in a white mess.
The seeds within red hot with sin,
penetrate deep below the skin.

This incredible happening
ever better
shadowed blue
and shying from the scree.

I thought I lost the urge

I thought I lost the urge
to invest,
> rhythm,
>> or merge.

Until I held the glance
of a dragon,
whose blood shed I wear.

Struck this soldier with such infectiousness
I dare not test
what remaining feistiness
I pray I may have left.

Upon the next dawn of day,
only callousness will feed
our growing tumour of matted grey.

Your lover...

I was your lover, in disguise;
Got the devil between my thighs.

I've left your soul distorted
and yet our worlds collided.

I'm fading to a sleaze
and I'm smoking eternity.

There's a painting off the wall
marking my grave of emptiness,
so many marks of helplessness.

A halo surrounds

A halo surrounds
you and your cello,
and the sweetest of suites
envelopes me mellow.

Crimson thoughts
control my mind
and I stand up, only to fall behind.

Speech impaired
from quivering lips
by the sounds emitted,
from within your hips.

Just you and your cello
and I,
a mellow fellow.

I scratch my chin
and glow within
'cause I'm just a mellow fellow.

Give me some death

Give me some death
at this time of night.
Paint red
the thoughts
scorched with lead.
Propose the rising,
cease the night
hear the music
learn to fight,
slump back
to watch
dying stars
burn bright.

This is the windy city

This is the windy city.

We have powdered drapes
like parked cars
stagnant.

Like crocodiles eating,
like armadillos.

We've found crazy people talking
and bumblebee candles burning,
inherit the night.

The T.V. (television) regains its composure
shouting nil
and a clock of no time,
maintains a steady beat.

We have a place of finely woven sheets
and the breath of cheesy feet.

Our daughter lies naked
as the city murmurs
beneath her sleep.

Why do I feel?

Why do I feel shit?
So much hurt.

I felt loved before,
                but that is no more.

Before I die out
I think I'll exit,
to where hurt won't be a factor,
anymore.

I must arise

I must arise,
leave this musty bed.

I must endure
what this day brings forth.

For what appears sad and lonely
often leaves
glad and only.

I'm being eaten

I'm being eaten
by a thousand flies.
Revenging the death
of many of their kind.

I am little,
sweet hell divine.
This MONSTROSITY
be so unkind.

The only war I see

The only war I see
behind closed eyes.
Where noise is void
in this shape sorting haven.

Tears all the same
scream out of here
& we find ourselves
at a junction,
of all that matters,
no more
no less
& a wrong decision,
detest
protest.

Makes me want to cry*

She makes me want to cry.
I've smelt her love
as she exits the room.

Crowned with her passion
swinging the night
sheltered in springs,
showered with light.

I've been drunk on her thoughts,
festive alone
& listened to music,
her voice on its own.

I have taken her hand
and kissed it goodbye
(&) many times now
she makes me want to cry.

*Written in Ilse's diary before we parted ways in Buffalo, New York, August 1999.

Book Two

This windy city

Here, within this windy city
a rosy haired lass,
struggles with a guitar.
                Alone.

Moments ago,
she was a rock goddess
adored by the thousand.
Now, as heavy clouds roll towards us,
the music ends.
Rock goddess status, ends.

Rusty

Rusty,
rusty and depressing this building opposite me.
It feeds my rusty writings
so much they require
a fair chunk of polish.
Polish and oil.

This formula of soberness proves fruitful.
I knew this, yet
I overlooked this conundrum.

W/a sigh

W/a sigh so massive,
it blows,
unseen dust particles off the table and into the air.
A moan of utmost relief & pleasure.

The light,
I have seen
and with it,
what I can achieve.

For my next act, I present, my personal recipe
for a most delightful veggie burger patty,
written now for you.

Veggie Burger Patty

Mushroom - pan fried or raw

Carrots - grated

Kumara - sliced, roasted

Broccoli - small bits

Pumpkin seeds

Capsicum - red, grate the inside flesh

Spinach - wilted

Sesame seeds

Poppy seeds

Paprika

(Beetroot) - garnish

Garlic - roasted

Onion

Couscous

Egg (or substitute)

Combine everything, roll onto a floured bench, cut into shapes. Cook in a pan or on the barbecue.

Your rhymes

Your rhymes are tight,
yet my words are mightier.

This ain't no beef,
I'm here to battle.

You stay up all night,
when I can just jot 'em.

You brag about being unique,
and I laugh,
because your writing is clichéd
                like a bucket of bad rhymes.

The smell of ink

The smell of ink
and the scrape of pen
      on paper.

Poetry writes itself.

Love becomes now
& beauty for the ages.

An explosion casts a shadowed earth,
a water drop, a bottle pops,
a floorboard squeaks above us.

This page is small,
but my rollerball
flows fast.
With words I hear,
yes! Elation.

A silver cup
I drink from
it holds no youth,
it's no saviour.

Instead of blogs
of rhymes & odes
with a keyboard,
no words, just silence.

No tap-pity-tap
comes forth
but hand me a pen, it flows,
it stops not.

Poetry writes itself.

The smell of ink,
and the scratch of pen on paper.

A thousand years of technology,
of evolution & yet
our single greatest creation for the future,
is the simple task of putting pen
to paper.

Paper beneath pen,
scribbles & words & verbs a plenty.

It's these here words, these here scribblings that
make my life
mean the most, give me hope
for a future smothered with books and words and
pages.

Still here I am

Intro: Alas, NYC is still but a dream. Instead stifled am I in a deep dark valley surrounded by liars and fakes. I thought I knew what was real; I thought I knew the deal. Instead I got tricked, played the fool, suffered in silence, been nothing but a mule.

Strong currents whip past cliffs,
scurrying up all in its way except me.
Cool winds blow over junky rocks,
whipping cocaine sand hard.

Clearing the way,
but still I stand.
Nothing remains still here I am.

The hard clash of fate tries to drag me, push me, end this.
Instead, I grab paper & pen & write.

A heart filled with pain.
A creative blade cuts my insides,
but this only fills up pages.

This search resumes, a new town need I
with cute real girls,
no lies, no fake tease.

The temp it drops,
warm glow, too low,
large birds swoop loud.
Menacing and close.

Bumps on my skin,
salt on my chin,
doors now closed,
it's time to go.

Children seated

Children seated in a row,
the red hair compère squeaky cute.
Silence reigns as they leave the room,
distant voices, ghosts of young ones gone.

Wives and children and mothers and siblings.
The purpose;
The point;
The prophecy.
If this was war they'd be everything remaining,
bar soldiers
limbless;
Lifeless
left alone.

A round table

A round table,
a perfect blonde,
a stomping child howls in scorn.

A beating drum,
a soundtrack made,
a movie this creates.

A Chinese script,
no thoughts match this,
a red lantern abates.

Tall brunette
disappears fast,
lift doors close behind her.

This could go on for lines and pages,
but break time now has ended.

Pretending to read

Pretending to read, the scarred gent lay.
He dozed and flicked pages.
Words only befuddled him.
Dirty shoes on the couch;
my grandfather moans from beyond at such filth.

An awkward Indian couple chats, nervous.
My presence confuses them.
I add to their confusion
by staring and writing
now immortalised.
Another couple enters the room they now exit; her
laugh contagious.

Unseen I stand in Escher's real world
with colours hanging from the roof or stairs.
People coming, different ones going,
neither seen again.
I count the contorted lines between levels —
a verisimilitude of vines and towers.

Too many, too confusing,
I could count all day, but I lose count
so I stop.

Too many books to read,
too many books piled high.
I see now why those Nazis and Christians burned
mountains of words,
it's easier to think without them.

Invisible

Invisible, she slept.
Jacket, couch and wall, super black.
In the shadow of the stairs, she dreamed.
What if I cuddled her?
Caressed her forehead - stroked her brow,
smoothed her curly hair.
My belly a soft pillow.
A gentle gesture by a nobody.

Awake.

Dreams broken,
thoughts in disarray.
A gaze empty now firms my place.
A stranger
whose stories dangle in the air.

Shape shifting stairs

Shape shifting stairs flowing up and gushing down whilst ghostly shadows bang and haunt the night.
Screeching nails on metal, whimpering cries and witchery laughs.
The dead haunt my days, but 'tis the nights I fear most.
When you're the only one;
The living one, the breath of life in decay.
You hide from it, keep quiet beside it, close your eyes lest they reflect your secret place.

In my garden I see words, beautiful, stemming from husky bark creating a forest of word trees shading me, protecting me.

Comforting words flutter my way as
a kiss of afternoon whispers rattles branches.

Letters float to the floor.
Heavy air weighs my lids and pushes my head to the fore.

Today it's empty

Today it's empty.
A purple cushion sits
fluffed up, patient,
awaiting a fellow body.

Black couch
with greasy leather
overused curvature.

Imagine the thousands of bottoms
that created the dent.
Bodies strewn across animal scents,
fingernails scratch the faux couch skin.

Blondes, redheads and brunettes, Africans and
Asians too.
Sleeping, not reading, eating and breathing.
I'd lounge there, but maybe I'll catch a disease.

It's softer than it looks,
the faint odour of ten thousand sweats, farts and bleeds.
I feel trapped can't move like a coma,
glued.

I risk losing limbs to escape and as I walk away a gay man sits in my chair and sniggers at what he thinks is luck.

Water smashing

Waterfall smashing tender moss braids,
droplets escaping mist it creates,
tendrils of webs whisper gently, my darling.

Cold stone numbs.
Pains like whips and cackles.
It may be sunny,
it may be cloudless, but you won't see it sans me,
much like the shadows where I hide.
You now remain.
Crouch down,
you cry.

Where is the jewel in this afternoon room?
Just two moments before it was my scene.
It's too late, I'm gone.

Ancient leaves twisted

Ancient leaves twisted round opal steeds.
Gnats biting my thumb and cheek,
blood tickles my toes.
The heat unbearable, stifles every pore,
till I'm thick with sweat. Itchy bumps scratched
raw, awkward and sore.

In polished lands, I seek gold
but it's these twisted greens that strike awe
for being strategic in their chaos.
A thousand trickling stories scream.

Blackbird bobbing, no two, wait, now three
following paths of definitive decree.
Skinny toes draw on new lumber
atop broken boulders crushed.
Falling leaves slipped between gaps in the wood.

Looking at the moon

Looking at the moon
big square dark room.
Masculine narrator,
a woman enters —
I ask to enter her,
she declines.

A palm tree
next to a lighthouse.
A devil's breeze
I admire this place.

It could house over fourteen thousand bodies
flat-stacked and piled high.
Would the UN allow such an expansive, white-walled room for just a video screen, a bench seat and no light?

Black drop.

Flowered wall

Flowered wall with a picture weeps.
Silence, but for thunderous roars of murderous rage.
Nought but a soul entertains,
just a flittering twig,
a bare branch,
a stone statue of a fair maiden
keeps watch over a trestle, green.
White doves in a cage and two cypress mark the
horizon; The furthest reach of my screams.

I came here to write, but wooden floors hurt my feet.
Silence deafens my thoughts,
flowered walls confine me
and murderous roars I fear.

I creep from room to room,
afraid I'll waken the old couple downstairs.

Waiting till I fall asleep
to take my liver, my life and words
to keep.

Short cube

Short cube
no light but that what's made.
Tiles yellow lengthen the room,
so, this is solitary confinement?
I don't mind, in here it's quiet.
I can think and breathe,
outside, it's alive and free.
Beating drums, this is how you welcome me?
I'm no saviour, but no devil eyes stare at you either.
Burning wood and childish chants;
A mini fern speaks of fear and trauma.
It quivers. I stomp its soul.

Lips dry

Lips dry,
arms heavy,
mellow my sense of self.

Gravity is strong today she says,
"no rockets taking off at least a week."
I didn't ask, but am told anyway.

Spotlights causing shadows,
direct eyes to random sides.
It's just a reflection; no need to fear them.
I count them regardless.

I'm disappointed by the exhibition, left empty by its lack of objects.
I think of my own photographs, words and movies.
It kills me knowing I should be there.
I have more to offer, my visions, powerful.
My words on canvas worthy of any gallery,
particularly this one.

Lovely little thing

Lovely little thing through the crowd.

Pink lips,
dimples,
twisting her ringlets.
Smiling,
sweetness
with eyes of Asian, but she is not.

She looks at me, but doesn't see.
She sees me eyeing her but doesn't budge an inch.

I get up to speak
but before I tread
she moves,
she's gone.

My heart tremors

My heart tremors,
my breathing short
furrowed are my brows.

3 doors with locks and handles,
the annoying kind makes me unsatisfied just seeing
them.

They are glass, but I can not see through them.
Black panes, a jail cell
I'm on the outside, stuck.

Couples languish in the sun,
cross-legged and in love.
Looking smug and on the cusp
of everything I have not.

I lay back below in awe and pity and close my eyes
and imagine it was better than what I see and feel,
and instantly it seems to fit —

This holy life I'm said to live this even smells just like a verse but it's just some words spat out with angst and none of this adds up to some kind of twist.

A simple sonnet explored within; My mind is best left within my brain.

Ostracised

Ostracised for the land I was born,
hated for the man I've become.

Bearded, a small patch of blue
in a crowd of white.

Wind swept talons of fair muddy grey
weed out the low, weak, lonely leaf
                        in this vagrant ghost town.

The soul remaining; me.
Not even ghosts bother here.

Broken trees,

                dead leaves,

                            and silence.

The theatre,
no shows —
depressing rough orange walls,
I hate the feel;
I hate the colour;
I hate it all.

Storm clouds swallow this street as I long for you,
just me,
it always is.

It won't be
as lonesome as this, forever.

I keep telling myself.
But I'm not convinced.

The red zone

It's late, no stars.
I count six buildings
not a light amongst them.

Graffiti stained windows
separates the abandoned from the dead.

Plastic tarps drumming the base line,
tension builds as the city breathes.

I expect zombies at every corner,
not a soul emerges,
not even their shadows.

A crumb filled Starbucks plate balances delicately
for years.

Streetlights red for no cars
disco beats drift on the winds.

Pretty reflections cast off muck filled holes
where once stood tall office buildings
and monuments grand.

The sole survivor
trips on a bump in the road.
Brittle leaves cackle and shimmer behind him.

Red glow on red bricks
screams porn and murder and lies and terror.

Hotel curtains speak of life.
It's false, just a white cotton breeze,
a smoke-filled breath
or an avenue of delirious shame.

Every step crunches, the only life remaining.

It may be broken, they may be blue,
this city of cross beams and struggle.

A patchwork of cracks and spaces,
some new, others forced.
A green thing stands tall.

I never took to this southern town,
flat and endlessly quiet.
I see it now
it's soul bared fresh,
thrust up a powerful fist.

It's the greenery that matters now.
Let it grow,
so too
you will follow.

Half-baked face

Every touch a sting,
every gust, bitter.
Thick winters eve, and unlike this land, its caress
tolerates us.

It's not that we're unreasonable, or greedy with our
requests,
of a sleep-filled night,
a belly full and to wake once more tomorrow.

The horizon, a dull haze
along with a dusty path to freedom.
Screaming drones flash above us,
machine-guns rat-a-tat-tat,
the same scenes drawn by brother's
a millennium ago.

Cultures long since discarded
by demigods, delivering blunt, crushed dreams.

Quick-witted flickering shadows seen
                              to tempt insecure flaws,

out here, hidden in the woods,
midnight roads announce passing ghosts.

Tendrils of webs sparkle as delicate jewels,
green scents engulf us,
safe from the noses of dogs trained to hate us.

Her tiny baked face shies away from my bamboo claw,
frail streams of fear melt over quivering lips.
A whisper,
weeping rock,
a gunshot in the night.

The cooler grasp of wrath,
as flat-packed starlets span the sky.

They're laughing way above us,
from distances immense.

Fighting one and other over precious lines declared
by men,
the triviality of lines drawn up long ago.

Invisible to all without a map,
unseen by screaming children dying.

Lake Hindmarsh

In the middle of a lake
without water,
cracked earth once tickled
with wind and tides.

Weeds and branches drift in,
afternoon breezes,
sunlight wafts and weaves its way through
thin clouds and thick.

My grandma once swam in this lake.
Now flat lands,
whimpering grass
whisper in the wind
of luxuries, long forgotten —

and dreams washed away
evaporated as the waters which never visit here,
anymore.

It's not change,
but death.
Life we know
has now ended.

And folk tales told as fairy tales
and hearsay belong in the clouds
that tease and mock
her open arms.

The first people here,
no, not the white ones
those that know the land
and caused it to… never mind.

Stories forgotten,
their words lost,
form no memory here.

Words disappeared with the waters that once filled this lake.

It's dusty, it crackles,
tiny birds chase insects buzzing in the grass
and I standalone,
drowning in the silence,
gasping in the sparseness.
My words, the last remaining memory of this place.

A cliff top

A cliff top
      this time, a beginning
instead of the end.

Flushed amber rocks lead one's eye to a blue
horizon.

Silence broken,
tap-pity tap on the roof
as a distant storm
reminds you, it will be here soon.

Birdcalls echo.
Shrill chirps and chatter
fall as invisible drops.

Clouds rise as smoke
from the valleys beneath me.
I'm the only human, as always.

Two letters scratched into
a blackened picnic table;
the only hint
someone's been here.

An ocean of trees stands still.
I'm sure it's teeming with life
but from way up here,
it's desolate.

The green/blue swollen hills
stacks of creatures
      long since dead.

I write ten thousand poems,
alone,
in the bush.
It's mundane, but it's my life.

I long to escape the drab,
the people, the noise and the horror.
I long to find immense journeys
      far from the clouds, adrift.

Just when I think I've found that place,
someone arrives,
clanking gears and swearing.

A glistening eucalypt
cracks a menacing haze
and a single cumulous
draws one's gaze.

Thunderstorm blues

An ethereal glow, post thunderstorm blues.
The forest comes alive
as six clocks tick tock out of sync.

I can't stop
counting droplets on windows
where streaks spell out words
written by tiny fingers at knee height.

A message for the future?
From gods to plebs,
a looking glass to the past.

It's argued, proposed—time travel is fake,
that no one has come or gone.
Take a trip of the mind,
memories make it real.

Begone thunderous rain,
heave stratus apart.

Baby pink candy-floss
lures lovers,

strangles poets
and dangles
forever in mist.

It's fleeting,
I'm too late,
like every female lover,
she's gone.

Silvery fingers scratch their persistence,
etching hate filled tears.
The outside creeping inside, bringing darkness with it.

The rain now drips.
Smoke wafts from the kitchen
and the last thing I see;
A jacaranda frond silhouetted against the sky,
quivering as blue turns to grey turns to black.

In a hate filled world

In a hate-filled world,
I have nothing but love
for her.

People wander aimlessly,
their faces drawn
blankly.

Missing her
& everything the world
has to give.

Crazy, deep water-filled beats
take over
drowning out the cars
this city, and the meek.

Left of the park
instead of trees,
a stump, a skeleton.

Its thick elephant toes, a statue of death;
Something that should have brought love
beneath its wide open arms.

We're told to dream

We're told to dream
our thoughts become real.
It's lies & fabrications.

Everything is false.

We're pawns in a kaleidoscope.
Stars dropped
on earth
for no purpose.

We're a mistake!

Look to the past, your future
with no singular answer,
just more fabrications
and lies,
more fake news;
not even a gorgeous smile to occupy my mind.

I'm told I'm loved,
but she's with another
and I sit with a pen,
the only thing to hold;
My purpose, love, and life.

I long for sweet kisses

I long for sweet kisses,
whispers in the night.

I ache for warmth,
her touch divine.

I can dream, create or wonder —
convince my brain otherwise.

We all know it's a trick,
a mind-control thing.

You can come, you can stay
you can say you'll be there.

There's only one chair, though.
We both know it's mine.

I'd love to share my thoughts,
whisper through your hair,

but that will never happen,
not in this lifetime, never.

The refugee

It wasn't her fault; they made her that way.
Fraught with blood-shed discombobulated eyes;
risen like a wild storm.

She heard rain when there was none.
She saw lights when it was dark.
She felt your warmth, even though you were on a
distant plain.

There was nothing she knew,
yet she knew it all.

They pumped her full of lies,
till she could remember no more truths.

She knew it wasn't real, none of it was, but she had
no proof.
Not a leaf, a penny, nor a dew drop of mystique.

She unfurled corners of dog-eared books,
hoping to find a singular hair, a thumbprint,
a lipstick kiss. There was nothing but space,
        a breath of salted air.

 In the cell next door, a smelly, rambling beatnik
        sprouted facts of life. No one would
listen. His words lost to the air.

She wonders if she'll ever see hope again.
Dangling from the cliff edges, hanging on for
dearest love.

It's that same old feeling,
a dancer amongst the drapes.
Hidden from the world.

Her beauty, her breath,
a languid love affair with life.

But nothing ever seems real,
because nothing ever was
Not this house, that cloud,
not even this right here.

A piece of paper with a signature,
the only thing real.
A key to a new world, a life imagined, a wonder-
filled daily dance.

A few cents worth of tree
becomes the epitome of perfection.
Leaving behind the crumpled, lost, and forgotten,
refugee.

I starve

I starve myself
to free my thoughts.

Add a pen & I become
the most powerful man in the world.

Adrift on endless bliss.

A soldier shooting empty cases,
    a bear lost in the woods
        unable to source its food or love,
           locked out of its den.

You and me,
we could do this or that,
or
we could have fixed everything,
instead, we're nothing
soulless, loveless, lifeless.

Empty thoughts of endless dreams
floating forever
in clouds of grey.

Cliff tops*

Clifftops
heavy air bundles up from the valley,
bringing with it —
the sweat & sleepless nights of ten thousand workers,
plying the fields.

Eucalyptus wafts between arched limbs,
just as her heavy scent trails behind;
Her cries of heartfelt destitution,
a death-rattle.

Up here,
clouds are spies.
Listening
to all your secrets,
before disappearing across the sky.

Unable to contain themselves.
Your lies, your hidden thoughts —
now scribbled along the horizon.

Their false innocence a dirty rag,
bloodied with the filth of a hundred slaves;

Of dollars,
perpetual numbers,
of ancient beaded necklaces once traded for land
filled with gold.
Now worthless, like the land that crafted them.

Land so polluted insects
can't find a reason to stay.
Just like me.

*There's lots of cliff tops in the Blue Mountains, hence why it features in multiple poems.

Memories tainted

Memories tainted,
they forget the horrors.

The rotting kelp,
biting sandflies,
bitter winds, dry earth
and water too rough for swimming.

I recall peace,
solitude
and never ending coastline.

Atop 253 steps. By a lighthouse, I stand.
White noise of crashing waves,
a blaring television tuned to no channel.

Unwavering grey clouds rise
from the ocean.

There's plenty of life below the blue-green murky wash. So I'm told.

Waves following
any path to destruction
turning to puddles
before getting sucked into the ocean,
whilst the wind keeps things busy.

It'll all go on without me,
indifferent
to my absence,
impervious to my presence.

I could sink into the wild waves of Palliser
& no one would be wiser.
Naught would change,
the surges would continue,
regardless.

Fireworks

Few fireworks
lend me your name.

Shout across the sky
burst into colours;
flashing bright,
bursting light.

It's a misrepresentation
of love & life
for none of it alive,
none found here.

Hanabi or flower fire
much better suited
for the beauty of petals
soon turn the fire to pain.

I'm told it's not true
that somewhere it's real.

But I've searched the world,
and I found nothing,
not an ounce of love,
barely a skerrick anywhere.

W/clouds

As clouds are my witness,
so too, they're my saviour.

Caressing my thoughts
and following me always.

Splendid and soft,
deep enough to capture my words.

W/clouds I feel protected,
surrounded by love,
they're always watching over me
unless the sky has none

A cloudless day
is a sad day for all.

No ears to listen, eyes to watch
or hands to hold.

Only an emptiness throughout the world.
Clouds be my saviour, my friend,
my love.

Christmas in New York*

I've had Christmases near and far,
one Christmas I spent on a cruise ship,
another thigh deep in snow,
just below the Finnish North Pole.

I've spent a Christmas in Japan,
another year in New Zealand.

But no holiday time was greater
than the Christmas
in New York.

It was everything I had dreamed of,
from the Santas to skating in Central Park.
No other time of year is merrier,
than Christmas in New York.

Christmas time in New York is a —
magical time of year.

It's even better than Times Square for New Year,
autumn or summers cheer.

Have a merry jolly Christmas,
in ole New York City.

Oh, it's full of sparkle, and tinsel,
lights on every street.
It doesn't matter if you're Buddhist or Muslim or Jewish,
it's a Happy Holiday treat.

Christmas time in New York is a special time of year.
No one Christmases like those,
New Yorker's can.

There's Santa's on 42nd Street,
carols in every store.

Even if it doesn't snow,
you'll find that in Macy's windows.

From the Christmas Tree at Rockefeller Place,
to the Rockettes at Radio City Music Hall.
It's all Christmas in New York.

Just like every Christmas movie,
from Jonathan and Sara, to Kevin and Elf,
it's serendipitous to be in New York,
alone or with someone else.

Like ice-skating in Central Park.
There's nothing so magical
as Christmas in New York.

Winter in the city, magic in the city,
this is Christmas in New York.

Christmas time, in New York is a —
magical time of year.
Full of sparkle and mystique,
carols and gingerbread.

From the first snow of Christmas Eve,
to the choir of St Paul's Cathedral.
Sipping spiced lattes
at outdoor markets, at Union Square place,
there's nothing magical as Christmas in New York.

Christmas time in New York is a —
special time of year.
There's no greater Christmas than a —
New Yorker year.

Even if you don't live there,
you can visit once a year;
If you're planning to go anytime,
I recommend going at Christmas time.

Oh, Christmas in New York is a —
magical time of year.
Christmas time in New York is —
full of joyous cheer.

There's no greater city to spend a Christmas in than
New York City it's the Christmassiest one.

Christmas time in New York is a —
magical time of year.
Full of winter's chill and sparkle,
carols and gingerbread.

There's no greater Christmas than a —
New Yorker one.
Christmas time in New York is a —
special time of year.

No one can Christmas like,
New Yorker's can.

Christmas time in New York is a —
magical time of year.

*For Jen xoxo

A wall

Before me stands a wall
of 32,000 cement bricks.

Weeds spill out the top,
proof light exists just ahead.
There's nothing to climb over it,
only the blanket of stratus clouds
disappearing over the wall;
to a land I'll never see,
a world I don't know,
a place I long to be
but will never reach.

I've searched for a ladder, a step,
a helping hand,
but none appeared.

I can only imagine
the gaiety and fanfare,

the warmth and love
on the other side.

I imagine it all at the bottom
of this grey stained wall,
too tall to escape.

I could knock it down,
chisel my way through
with no guarantee
I'll be welcome.

Vultures and crows circle
as I claw at the gritty cement wall
bare, mighty and frightful.

Imprisoned by thoughts
buried by grief,
stuck,
unable to breathe.

No one stops,
not a moment to capture; everyone keeps going
leaving me far behind.

None of it matters*

We spend our entire lives searching
                for that thing we're promised,
the one sensation that's supposed to rule all.

What if everything is wrong?
What if it doesn't exist?
There's zero purpose to this?

A rock, a leaf, a speck of sand.
There's more than love to these.

Notice the multitude of shades of green,
after the rain?
The deep rich burst of life,
the soft method of its sultry persistence
and branches dangling leaves like soft caresses
in the night.

A tree does not think, feel love or drink alcohol,
yet it is alive.

A solitary blade of grass does not tell jokes, eat
Thai food, or smile.
Yet it too is alive.

A flower sprouting pink and dripping scents of love
does not write poetry,
it has no need,
yet it's still alive.

What is life to trees, grasses, and flowers without
love,
a smile,
or sweet delicate poetry?

We surround ourselves
with their essence and beauty
because we're secretly jealous.
We long to be better;
assured it's for a reason.

We forget it doesn't matter.
None of it.
Not that person walking, or last night's leftovers.
Not a red shirt, instead of a blue one.
Not a castle overlooking a townhouse.

Nothing matters.
Nothing matters at all.

A star, a cloud, a whale's puff of steam squeaking and squawking through green seas.

None of this matters
if it disappeared.

Just like you and me
and every green tree.
None of it matters.
Nothing at all.

*Written after Jennifer had died, but 12 days before I found out. Ironically it was also the day I sent my last message to her, thinking she was busy. The message read, 'did you survive the chill?' In reference to the polar vortex that hit Chicago a few days before. Jennifer Olsen died on the 21st January, 2019. The following poems were written in the days, weeks and months of grief and confusion.

The box

A box arrived,
            small yet filled.
Full of history,
            mysteries,
hope, love & answers.

I've kept my life at bay,
refused to move onward,
waiting for this box.

Now it's here, tainted
with the sweat of other men.
I'm too scared to open it.

I've held it, sniffed it, stroked it
and turned it.

Is it your last gift, or a letter?
It's the memories I fear the most.

Stories of our love, passion;
Our short trysts in foreign cities
holding hands & exploring
bustling alleys, the rooftops of skyscrapers & the
                         gentle caresses on boats.

Our last ever trip,
not even a goodbye.
I want this box to never end
because the moment it's opened,
you're gone, our story ends.

It's now a box of tears
awaiting release.

It lacks your warmth,

                 your…

I know it's from you
but it also contains you—a hat, a shirt. I imagine
your pleasurable scent drifting through a crack in
the seal.

The proof you're gone, I need,
but I don't want to accept,
so—I look at the box instead.

I expected answers

I expected answers,
                there's none.

Only reminders of our love,
                long gone.

Not even her smell attached.
A few scattered remains
of a life lived—now ended.

I yearn to cry, to hold her,
to speak once more.

I'm empty,
nothing left.
Not a sign,
      a symbol,
           or words of hers to comfort my soul.

Inside, I'm dead,
just as she is,
since the 21st of Jan, 2019.

A blanket of softness

A blanket of softness,
a glowing speck of orange,
a ragged line that should be straight.

Clicks, chirps and whistles echo all around us.
On a mountaintop,
above it all,
crisp morning sentiments
stumble.

The show has begun;
her warmth, her mere presence,
eradicates thoughts.

Like meditation,
a blank mind equals a quiet life,
without sadness.

It's never silent.
Her drumbeat, a snare,
sweaty fingers play on.

The show continues
    regardless
of you watching,
or even being here.

It hurts to think

We're here,
she's not,
it hurts to think;
more so, solo.

A single line
is all my worth,
without words from her.

Silence we crave
unless it's forced
or born from anger,
mismatched love
or torn from weather.
Dreams broken,
futures uncertain,
love unknown.

A February I'll always remember
not for its warmth

but the death of my love,
my heart, my crushed soul.
A day I dreaded, a day forlorn.

Should have been a Mrs

My heart aches,
stomach in twists and knots —
You're all I envision.

Deep sadness fills my days,
missing you immensely.

A love unfulfilled,
a future now gone.

I could fill a novel, with the things I miss about you,
I wish I didn't have to.

A bliss I'll never know;
      A Miss who should have been a Mrs;
Our last kiss, long savoured,
now remembered.
Love torn in two by death.

It should have been a saga for the ages,
instead, it's a novella;
the last dozen pages ripped
                                      and torn,
unread,
        untold.

Gone from my days

In a grassy field
      pockmarked with invisible faces
            by the thousands.
Surrounded by death, tall trees and tinsel flapping
on tiny white crosses,
stuck haphazardly in the ground.

It should scare me,
      but it's peaceful.

I should be angry,
      but here,
          beneath wispy clouds and shimmering
leaves,
      I'm relaxed.

Gone from my days,
      oh sweet delicate one,
her life failed by all.

She didn't belong in this world,
                      of anger, hate, and madness.

She felt everyone's pain,
                      stacked on top of her own.

It was all too much.
        Like the princess
        and the pea,
no amount of softness could hide the torment inside her.

She felt everything,
        including thoughts by you,
        and me.

I want to wrap her up in my arms and hold her tight, forevermore,

leaving no breath unsqueezed,
no blink untethered,
no heartbeat missed.

    I loved her;
    she knew it;

                                         I think.

    I'm sure she
held onto me for as long as she could.

There should have been many things;
        instead there's just
        a handful of photos
from love-filled nights in
    Sydney | San Fran | New York | Fort Worth.

The rest memories;
        which, one day, I'll forget.

Her death shocked me,
        as receiving a terminal notice;
though with no such poison released,
        only I remain.

I always thought fate would join us,
        but it never did,
it lied,
        deceived us as the devil who makes
twisted stories become the entrails of forgotten
dreams.

One less conversation.
                My phone beeps less now.

Messages stay unread,

                and will forevermore.

A dent in the dirt

Her long established frailty
cruelly disposed of in a world untoward.

She's an inconvenient reminder,
her story,
a failure of many.

I often dream of escape;
to disappear off-grid,
unattached to the digital realm.

Where painters and roadsters and other damned
traits survive, lost, forgotten…

Her life less remarkable.
Did she plan her escape?

Solitude,
dank in the darkness,
her breath left warmth
whilst her words trailed into nothing.

Black musty sleeping bag
warming those few scraps of cardboard;
a dent in the dirt where her body once lay.

A dent in the dirt
of a life half-lived.
Pain embedded in her DNA;
unfixable.

There were others clutching sandwiches
dozing away,
eyes unblinking,
teeth chattering,
legs bent,
bodies strewn in awkward stances.

A day and another
her life ended
theirs, bland indifference.
Seeking a puff of smoke,
a capful of ale
or a dollar for a toothy grin.

A quick hit, more tempting than her lifetime
of love,
thoughts or words
to warm our breath each night.

Once a purpose lay

Six months of silence,
a year (or more) since our last conversation.

I've seen the cold, cruel clutch of death before,
but this time,
it's absolute.

Where once a purpose lay,
solid on our path.
Now hope - that dastardly word,
four letters that rule kingdoms,
change politics
and allow slavery to continue.

Hope ceases to be,
it has no purpose here.
Hope is worse than a god,
it takes our lives
and gives nothing in return.

Where once a solid path
led us over the hills,
now it's crumbled,
its signs have fallen.

Hills have become mountains,
valleys filled with the raging tears of hope,
lost.

Warmth disappearing over falls
onto the cold
solid rocks
below.

Worn smooth from years
of torment gushing over them,
leaving a rock,
                too,
without hope

of ever becoming
a mountain.

Across the ether

Across the ether
of our love, divided.

Her warmth ceased;
no clouds remain.

Blue skies silent
except for the planes
taking everyone
some place else.

Everyone but me.

I used to roam.
I used to…

Now I wander haphazardly.
I used to travel;
I used to live stories; now I tell them.

A pocket of wildness

A pocket of wildness between two worlds anew,
a border discarded,
where neither side claims ownership.

Few regions of the world remain lost,
where one can escape, yet here I am.

I chuckle and smile at having disappeared.
No bar exists to track me down.

A fleeting glimpse, that lasts two breaths.
The chortle of tweeting parakeets
serves a solid, shrill reminder.

They're always watching,
forever listening;
I'll never be alone
with my thoughts
nor forgotten,
until I'm gone.

We know nothing

We say we hear the wind,
kissing, smothering, howling,
but it's not.

It's paper rustling in a breeze,
leaves gossiping in dim-lit alleys.
It's tree-trunks moaning,
and sheets of metal shivering throughout the night.

Every tree branch throw's its arms
              recklessly towards blue cloudless skies.
No one question's its motives
fewer mock its design.

We think we know everything,
that we're right.

Yet it's clear
we're mocked behind closed doors.

We know nothing,
and all we know
is wrong.

With each heavy breath

With each heavy breath,
a life less.

With every second more
stories drift ever further from you.

Your life that now exists,
remains in words
told by others.

A lifetime of love, food, shopping, travel, family
and heartache.

At the end, your life or mine,
it's all the same —
a heavy heart,
a deep breath
and a sigh.

If you could pick the soundtrack,
what last song
would you choose?

A ballad? A foxtrot? A Broadway musical?
When we're done,
no dollars, no house, no car or lover
saves us from the end.

You could choose ten thousand choices —
you could bury treasure, starve yourself, travel,
eat burgers or lettuce; matter it does not.

We all end up in the same place.

You could wear dresses or pants,
short hair or black,
six kids or none.

We still end up in the same place.

You could plant flowers, succulents or shrubs,
you could grow cotton, lamb, or wear hijabs.

We're all the same once we're dead.

The end is but a minute passing,
an hour gone
without a breath, a heartbeat or a blink.

Micro story #1

Estelle slumped into her grey velvet armchair. Outside, a bee buzzed and flitted amongst flowers.

A bloodied tissue lay crumpled in her hand. It was all that remained from her marriage.

His sweat clung to her, his last grip she'd soon wash away. Estelle was now free; to travel, eat cake, or dance without fear.

Her daughter screamed, "no Daddy, no." Her cries drifted ever further, opening wounds from her last kiss.

"What is freedom without her?" Estelle blubbered.

Golden bottlebrush flowers stroked against her bedroom window in the afternoon breeze.

The bee flew away, the pollen, gone.

Micro story #2

Water splashes as hard clumped beads; clanging metal as she tried to sleep.

The nights were troublesome. Shadows stood still, waiting for a glimpse of skin; white, soft, and velvety. Her nakedness, a fragility, whilst clothes imprisoned her.

His touch, a long-forgotten fantasy.

Walls creaked and whispered in jest. She wriggled and writhed in waken agony.

Her thoughts, violent struggles; every night, she saw her death. It was tortuous.

The dark silence of a village war cry, which always ended the same. The darkness would cower, disappear for a while, leaving birds to chirp in place of the walls.

Micro story #3

Two gents sprouting whiskers from yonder the hills. Wearing panther-black jeans and leather boots, smelly and stiff. Wooden soles clunked on rocks, like sticks on a bass drum.
One had beef, the other none.

Two guns drawn, along with a knife; slashing and shooting under the fading sun.

Death came to both men. It was their determination, their hatred of life, that enabled this useless end; Two lives wasted.

A daughter and a wife stood shaking. They both hugged and wept.

Thirsty flies gathered, sipping from dusty pools of blood.

Two lives disappeared, what's left, all that matters.

Micro story #4

No one heard the screeching tyres, smashing glass or crunching metal.

She did everything right—seatbelt, no phone, and eyes on the road; Sober, a slow driver, and worked hard at school.

He was drunk, using his phone, and dropped out of school.

Her perfect organs saved none; his heart, eyes, and kidney now belong to three other lives. They become a doctor, a foster parent, and a teacher of love.

Death comes for everyone, sometimes sooner than later. All deaths are useless, but not all lives have to be.

Everyday now, a solo mother cries, empty.

Micro story #5

Stubble tickled her neck; aftershave, wooden and seductive. His last gift, dark-red and trickling. Better than his black and yellow ones.

Her smile became laughter through tears… followed by a sigh.

"One wrong choice," she sobbed.

In another timeline, her legs dangled over a pier; cool splashes tickle her toes as pink clouds filled skies with love.

Instead she shuffled, the linoleum squeaked, her chains clanked like beats in a song. Leather and bleach merged with neon lights, bright. The last memory of a life unjust.

Darkness edged on a tiny wooden cross, who's writing would fade without love.

The End

Afterward

Thank you so much for reading *Drunk Love Sober Death*. If you would like more of my writings, head to my website, https://jadejackson.com.au where you can find my play, *Compass* along with a novella, articles and more.

If you loved this book, please tell your friends, leave a review on the site you purchased this book from, or if you have feedback, you can send me an email at https://jadejackson.com.au/contact.

Visit: https://jadejackson.com.au/subscribe to be notified about future published works.

Check out my podcasts:
Jade Talks Travel
Jade Talks Cheap Flights
Jade Talks Stuff
Available wherever you get your podcasts from,

including Apple Podcasts, Google Podcasts, Spotify, Radio Public, and my website.

You can find me on:
Twitter: @jadekinsjackson
Facebook: @jadekinsjackson
Instagram: @jadekinsjackson
Reddit: @jadekinsjackson

If you would like to purchase custom designed, poetry themed merchandise including shirts, stickers or notebooks, check out:

https://bit.ly/JadeJacksonShop

Thank you for purchasing and reading this book. It means the world to me.

    - Jade Jackson

www.ingramcontent.com/pod-product-compliance
Lightning Source LLC
Chambersburg PA
CBHW030255010526
44107CB00053B/1726